PEARSON LANGUAGE CENTRAL

ELD Song Book

Grade 1

Glenview, Illinois • Boston, Massachusetts • Chandler, Arizona •
Upper Saddle River, New Jersey

Acknowledgments

Cover: Daniel Moreton

Unit R Week 1 Hector Borlasca; Week 2 Gabrielle Grimard; Week 3 Rob Hefferan; Week 4 Cecilia Rebora;
Week 5 Sue Williams; Week 6 Jan Bryan Hunt

Unit 1 Week 1 Jan Bryan Hunt; Week 2 Jane Smith; Week 3 Cecilia Rebora; Week 4 Hector Borlasca;
Week 5 Gabrielle Grimard; Week 6 Michelle Gengaro

Unit 2 Week 1 Michelle Gengaro; Week 2 Jessica Secheret; Week 3 Sue Williams; Week 4 Michelle Gengaro;
Week 5 Rob Hefferan; Week 6 Carolina Farias

Unit 3 Week 1 Red Hansen; Week 2 Jane Smith; Week 3 Hector Borlasca; Week 4 Jan Bryan Hunt;
Week 5 Gabrielle Grimard; Week 6 Rob Hefferan

Unit 4 Week 1 Carolina Farias; Week 2 Sue Williams; Week 3 Cecilia Rebora; Week 4 Red Hansen;
Week 5 Ariel Pang; Week 6 Michelle Gengaro

Unit 5 Week 1 Jane Smith; Week 2 Christopher Lyles; Week 3 Gabrielle Grimard; Week 4 Red Hansen;
Week 5 Carolina Farias; Week 6 Michelle Gengaro

ISBN-13: 978-0-328-39872-0
ISBN-10:   0-328-39872-1

Pearson® is a trademark, in the U.S. and/or in other countries, of Pearson plc or its affiliates.

5 6 7 8 9 10   12 11

CC1

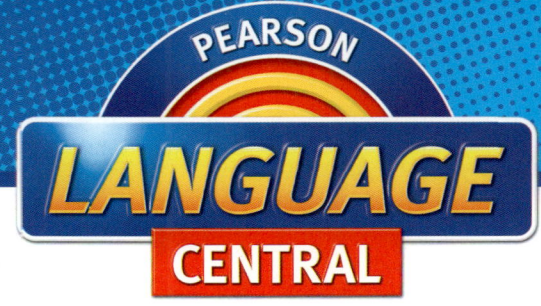

Table of Contents

Table of Contents continued

My Home

Tune: "Home on the Range"

I live in a place,
With a very nice space,
With a **bedroom**
Where I sleep and play.
It's pretty and **green,**
It is so nice and clean,
How I love being there
Every day!

Home, home is,
You **see,**
The place where
I most like to be.

My home's where I stay
With my family each day,
Home is my **favorite** place,
Just for me!

Who Is in a Family?

Tune: "The Eensy Weensy Spider"

Who is in a family?
Who may there be?
There may be Mom and Dad,
And a **baby** you may see.
There may be a sister,
Or a brother you may find.
A family lives **together,**
Each a different kind.

Who is in a family?
Who may there be?

There may be a **grandma,**
Or **grandpa** you may see.

They **care** for each other
And **like** each other, too.
We each have a family,
Yes, we all do!

Look Outside

Tune: "Three Blind Mice"

Look outside.
Look outside.
What do you see?
What do you see?
I see a **bird** up in a tree.
It looks as happy as can be.
It is a lot of **fun** when we
Can look outside!

Look outside.
Look outside.
What do you see?
What do you see?

I see the grass on the ground,
With **yellow flowers** all around,
There is so much that I have found.
Just look outside!

Question of the Week — What can we do with our neighborhood friends?

In Our Friendly Neighborhood

Tune: "This Old Man"

I see you, you see me,
We are happy as can be!
Let's be kind and let's be good,
In our **friendly neighborhood!**

See the **dog** on our street,
I like every pet I meet.
Let's be kind and let's be good,
In our friendly neighborhood!

Our **mail carrier** I can see,
With **two** letters just for me!
Let's be kind and let's be good,
In our friendly neighborhood!

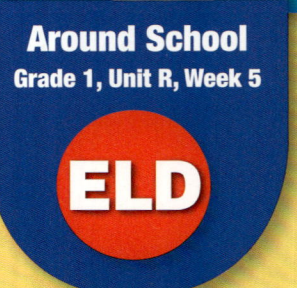

Around School
Grade 1, Unit R, Week 5

ELD

I Go to School!

Tune: "Skip to My Loo"

CHORUS:

School, school, I go to school!

School, school, I go to school!

School, school, I go to school!

I go to school to learn there!

In the **classroom,** it is fun.

There is a book for everyone.

I **read** a book about a yellow sun.

I go to school to learn there!

CHORUS

I take my **backpack** every day.
I like to work, I like to play.
My **teacher** helps in every way.
I go to school to learn there!

CHORUS

Come and See the Neighborhood

Tune: "Do You Know the Muffin Man?"

CHORUS:
Come and see the neighborhood,
The neighborhood, the neighborhood.
Come and see the neighborhood,
Let's **visit** places here.

Here's a **market** we can try.
Vegetables and **fruit** we'll **buy.**
I like this market, that is why
I visit places here!

CHORUS

Here's a park **where** we can play,
I hope that we can play all day.
I like this park, that's why I stay
And visit places here.

CHORUS

If You Had a Pet

Tune: "Do Your Ears Hang Low?"

If you had a **pet,**
What would it need to get?
Would you give it a home
To call its own?
What would you do
To make it **come** to you,
If you had a pet?

If you had a **cat,**
Would you pet it with a pat?
Would it get to stay
Where it **slept** all day?

Would you watch a **kitten** run
And let it have some fun,
If you had a pet?

The Vet

Tune: "Mary Had a Little Lamb"

If your pet is feeling **sick,**
Feeling sick, feeling sick,
If your pet is feeling sick,
Then **take** it to the **vet.**

Get your pet **examined** there,
Examined there, examined there.
Get your pet examined there,
You **want** to do it soon.

The vet may give you **medicine,**
Medicine, medicine.

The vet may give you medicine
To give to your pet.

Soon your pet will be all well,
Be all well, be all well.
Soon your pet will be all well,
Thanks to the vet!

Rescue, Rescue!

Tune: "Camptown Races"

Many dogs **help** people out,
Rescue, rescue!
Rescue dogs can go about
And find a person fast!

A **hiker** in the **woods** is **lost**,
Rescue, rescue!
Rescue dogs can run across
And find the hiker fast!

Using just their nose,
They **follow** each **scent**.

Soon they find the people lost,
They find just where they went.

In the Ocean

Tune: "My Bonnie Lies Over the Ocean"

The **ocean** is home to the **dolphins,**
The ocean is home to the **whales.**
But some **boats** that go in the ocean
Must watch for their backs or their tails.

CHORUS:
Help them, help them,
Protect those that live in the sea, the sea.
Help them, help them,
Protect those that live in the sea.

We must keep the ocean a **safe** place,
We must show that we really care.
We must keep the ocean a **clean** place,
So animals can be safe there.

CHORUS

Birds

Tune: "Row, Row, Row Your Boat"

Birds, birds, birds are here,
Birds are in the sky.
Flying, flying, flying, flying,
Oh, so very high!

Birds, birds, birds are here,
Birds are in the **tree**.
They make a **nest** upon a **branch**,
A nest for all to see.

Birds, birds, birds are here,
Birds are in their nest.

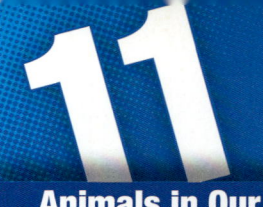

Soon an **egg** will hatch, and then
A new bird joins the rest!

Elephants

Tune: "Over the River and Through the Woods"

Over the ocean, across the sea,
To Africa we go!
We see an **elephant** with its calf,
And learn a lot, you know!
Over the ocean, across the sea,
To Africa we fly!
We watch the elephants in a **herd**
As they go walking by!

Over the ocean, across the sea,
To Africa we go!

We're each just like a **scientist,**
Who learns a lot, you know!
Over the ocean, across the sea,
To Africa we fly!
And once we've **studied** what is there,
We wave and say goodbye!

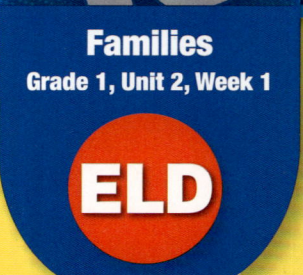

Family Is Fun

Tune: "Happy Birthday"

It's fun to have a **family,**
There is so much to do.
You **gather** with each other
And talk about what's new.

You gather for a **meal,**
And then when you are done,
You help to **wash** the dishes,
You help with everyone!

You gather when you're working,
You gather when you play.

I **think** my family is the best
Each and every day!

The People in Our School

Tune: "The Farmer in the Dell"

CHORUS:
The people in our school,
The people in our school,
They **make** our school a better place,
The people in our school.

The **principal** is here,
The school **nurse** is here,
They make our school a better place,
The people in our school.

The lunch workers are here,
The **janitor** is here,
They make our school a better place,
The people in our school.

CHORUS

At the Playground

Tune: "My Darling Clementine"

At the **playground,** there are **people,**
Many people working there.
Yes, the playground's **nice** and pretty,
That's because the people care.

Many people pick up **litter,**
So the playground will be clean.
Yes, the playground's nice and pretty,
And the grass is soft and green.

People **fix** things in the playground,
Anything that's broken there.

Yes, the playground's nice and pretty,
That's because the people care.

Question of the Week How do animal communities work together to survive?

16

Animal Communities
Grade 1, Unit 2, Week 4

ELD

Animal Communities

Tune: "Jimmy Crack Corn"

A lot of people find it's good
To live together in a neighborhood.
They're not the only ones that do.
Some animals live together, too.

CHORUS:

Animal **communities,**
Animal communities,
Animal communities,
Where animals live together!

Many animals can be found
Living together **under** the **ground.**
They dig a **hole** so deep and wide,
And in their homes, they're safe **inside.**

CHORUS

The Food Chain

Tune: "There Once Was a Man Named Michael Finnegan"

CHORUS:

Plants and animals need each other.
Plants and animals use each other.
Plants and animals help each other.
All are part of the **food chain**.

Frogs think that bugs are a treat.
They get **strong** from bugs they eat.
Bugs are food that can't be beat!
Bugs are part of the food chain.

CHORUS

Plants use animals that pass on.
Plants use animals once they're gone.
They use their bodies to feed on.
Animals are part of the food chain!

CHORUS

Question of the Week How is an insect community like a community of people?

18

Insect
Communities
Grade 1, Unit 2, Week 6

ELD

Insects

Tune: "Down By the Station"

See all the **insects,**
See them work together.
Insects work together
Just like people do.
Some make the home,
And some get the food.
Insects are like people,
They have jobs, too.

See the **hive** of **bees,**
They all work together.

The **queen** is the head
Over all the rest.
Some work in the hive,
And some make the food.
Then all of the bees
Return to the nest.

Things Change

Tune: "Are You Sleeping?"

Once a **building,** once a building
Was in town, was in town.
Now you cannot see it, now you cannot see it.
It was **torn** down, it was torn down.

Once some flowers, once some flowers
Grew right there, grew right there.
Now you cannot see them, now you cannot see them,
Anywhere, anywhere.

Things don't **always,** things don't always
Stay the same, stay the same.

Once we had old things, once we had old things,
Then new things came, new things came!

Grow Older

Tune: "There Were Ten in the Bed"

CHORUS:
We all grow up and **continue** to grow,
And as we get big, the more we know.
Grow older! Grow older!

We all grow older and learn a lot,
Like what is cold and what is hot.
Grow older! Grow older!

We all grow older **every** day,
We learn at work, we learn at play.
Grow older! Grow older!

As we grow older, how good it feels
To ride a big wheel with three **wheels!**
Grow older! Grow older!

As we grow older, how good it feels
To ride a **bicycle** with two wheels!
Grow older! Grow older!

CHORUS

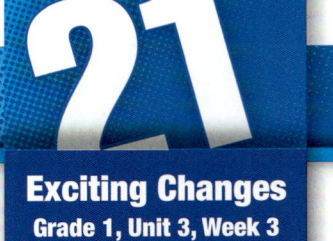

New Things

Tune: "Old MacDonald Had a Farm"

CHORUS:
It is fun to do new things,
New things can be fun!
At first you feel a little **scared,**
So does everyone!

In a new **school,**
You make new **friends.**
At first you're scared,
But then it ends.
It is fun to do new things,
New things can be fun!

In a new **house**
You look around,
See new places
You have found.
It is fun to do new things,
New things can be fun!

Weather Changes

Tune: "London Bridge Is Falling Down"

Drops of **rain** are falling down,
Falling down, falling down.
Drops of rain are falling down.
That's the **weather!**

Soon the dark **clouds** go away,
Go away, go away.
Soon the dark clouds go away.
That's the weather!

Now the sun is coming out,
Coming out, coming out.

Now the sun is coming out.
That's the weather!

Soon the rain is back **again,**
Back again, back again.
Soon the rain is back again.
That's the weather!

Around the Year

Tune: "If You're Happy and You Know It"

In the **spring,** many flowers start to **bloom,**
In the spring, many flowers start to bloom.
Many flowers all around
Start to **push** up from the ground.
In the spring, many flowers start to bloom.

In the summer, many flowers grow so tall,
In the summer, many flowers grow so tall.
Many flowers all around
Keep on growing in the ground.
In the summer, many flowers grow so tall.

In the fall, many **birds** fly away,
In the fall, many birds fly away.
Many birds fly away
To a warmer place to stay.
In the fall, many birds fly away.

In the winter, many things aren't around,
In the winter, many things aren't around.
But just **wait** for the spring.
See what warmer days will bring.
Birds and flowers will be back around the town!

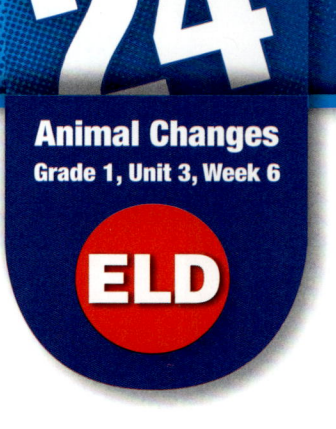
Before It Is Winter

Tune: "On Top of Old Smoky"

CHORUS:

Before it is winter,
Some animals go.
They **migrate** to places
Where they **won't** be cold.

The **geese** are all flying,
They fly **south** as one.
They migrate to places
Where there will be sun.

A **sea turtle** swims far,
For food and a nest
She goes to a beach
Then lays eggs and rests.

CHORUS

Surprises and Treasures

Tune: "Twinkle, Twinkle, Little Star"

Right before your very eyes,
You may find a big **surprise.**
It can be a **treasure,** too,
One that has a great **value.**
Treasures come in any size.
Large or small, a sweet surprise!

Treasures may be big or small,
Things you don't expect at all.
If a treasure came to you,
What do you think you **would** do?

Treasures come in any size.
Large or small, a sweet surprise!

Make a Card

Tune: "Three Blind Mice"

Make a **card.**
Make a card.
Make it for a friend.
Make it for a friend.
A card is so nice to **create.**
It's a treasure that is so **great.**
Make one now, don't sit and wait.
Yes, make a card!

I made a card.
I made a card,
For a sick friend,
For a sick friend.

I **drew** a **picture** of the moon.
I drew a pretty red balloon.
And then I printed, "Get well soon!"
I made a card!

Treasures in Our Country

Tune: "The Yellow Rose of Texas"

Our **country** is a treasure,
A treasure very grand.
We've **found** so many treasures
Across our special land.
Our **president** is a treasure
Who leads our country well.
Our country is a treasure,
So special, we can tell!

Our country is a treasure,
A treasure that we love.

Our **flag** is a **national** treasure
That proudly waves above.
It **took** a lot of hard work
To make our country great.
Our country is a treasure,
And so is every state!

The 4th of July

Tune: "I'm a Yankee Doodle Dandy"

There's a special day we treasure,
With **fireworks** in the sky.
What's the day we **celebrate?**
It is the 4th of July!

We march and sing about our country,
We wave our flag **above.**
It's our country's birthday!
July 4th, a day we love!

Treasures in a Home

Tune: "Home on the Range"

A family home
Is a very nice home.
When you visit,
You find treasures there.
A **family room**
Is a very nice room,
Where each **picture**
Is put up with care.

Home, home
Is a place
Where a treasure
Can have its own space.

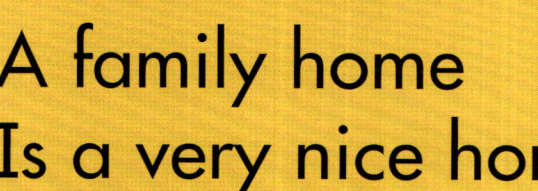

A picture can be
Something special to see.
It can put a smile
On your face.

Neighbors, Neighbors

Tune: "Daisy, Daisy, Give Me Your Answer, Do"

Neighbors, neighbors,
Please come across this way.
I have treasures
To share with you this day.

A **garden** of food I grew here.
I'm glad that I see you here.
Just pass the **gate,**
Come now, don't wait,
Because I've much to share.

Problem and Solution

Tune: "Are You Sleeping?"

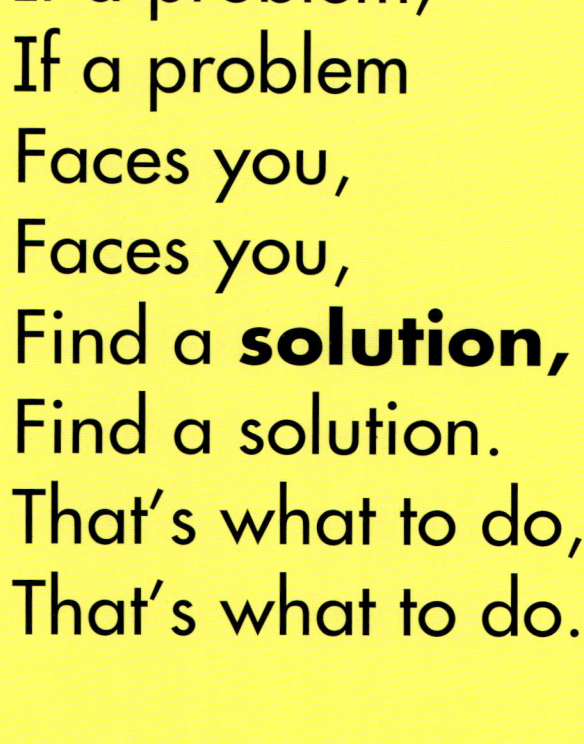

If a problem,
If a problem
Faces you,
Faces you,
Find a **solution,**
Find a solution.
That's what to do,
That's what to do.

End your problem,
End your problem.
Yes, but **how**?

Yes, but how?
A **clever** solution,
A clever solution
Will end it now,
Will end it now!

Question of the Week — How can we look at things in a different way?

32

New Ways to Do Things
Grade 1, Unit 5, Week 2

ELD

Try a New Way

Tune: "Oh, Dear, What Can the Matter Be?"

CHORUS:

Oh, dear, what can the matter be?
One big problem is facing me.
I tried to end it but can't you see.
Now I must try a new way.

My problem has **turned**
My day **upside down.**
I look to the **clouds,**
I look to the ground.

A clever solution
I have not found,
So now I must try a new way.

CHORUS

It's a Mystery

Tune: "Did You Ever See a Lassie?"

CHORUS:

Have you ever had a **mystery,**

A mystery, a mystery?

Have you ever had a mystery

You wanted to **solve?**

Have you **looked** for **clues?**

Good clues you can use.

Have you ever had a mystery

You wanted to solve?

CHORUS

For clues you might look
In a **closet** or **book.**
Have you ever had a mystery
You wanted to solve?

CHORUS

A Great Idea

Tune: "When the Saints Go Marching In"

CHORUS:
Oh, when you get a great **idea,**
Oh, when you get a great idea,
A lot of people can **enjoy** it,
When you get a great idea!

To get around so long ago,
To get around so long ago,
People had to ride on **horses,**
To get around so long ago.

Then someone had a great idea,
Then someone had a great idea,
And people got around on **bikes,**
The bike was such a great idea!

Then someone else used **gas** and **oil,**
Then someone else used gas and oil,
And people rode around in cars,
The car was such a great idea!

CHORUS

Question of the Week: How can a great idea change the way we live?

35

Ideas That
Change Lives
Grade 1, Unit 5, Week 5

ELD

New Things

Tune: "The Farmer in the Dell"

CHORUS:
New things have **changed** our lives,
New things have changed our lives.
Ideas have caused a lot to change,
New things have changed our lives!

A long time ago,
News traveled slow.
People sent **letters,**
And the **mail** traveled slow!

Then lots of time passed,
And news traveled fast.
People had **phones** to use,
And news traveled fast!

CHORUS

A Great New Idea

Tune: "On Top of Old Smoky"

CHORUS:

A great new idea
Can be lots of fun.
A great new idea
Can get a lot done.

You might **build** a **robot**
That has a great use.
It can **retie** your **shoelaces**
If they come **loose!**

And when day is over,
Your robot will know
How to **untie** your shoelaces
So to bed you can go!

CHORUS